A Versailles Christmas-Tide

By
Mary Stuart Boyd

A Versailles Christmas-Tide

CHAPTER I

THE UNEXPECTED HAPPENS

No project could have been less foreseen than was ours of wintering in France, though it must be confessed that for several months our thoughts had constantly strayed across the Channel. For the Boy was at school at Versailles, banished there by our desire to fulfil a parental duty.

The time of separation had dragged tardily past, until one foggy December morning we awoke to the glad consciousness that that very evening the Boy would be with us again. Across the breakfast-table we kept saying to each other, "It seems scarcely possible that the Boy is really coming home to-night," but all the while we hugged the assurance that it was.

The Boy is an ordinary snub-nosed, shock-headed urchin of thirteen, with no special claim to distinction save the negative one of being an only child. Yet without his cheerful presence our home seemed empty and dull. Any attempts at merry-making failed to restore its life. Now all was agog for his return. The house was in its most festive trim. Christmas presents were hidden securely away. There was rejoicing downstairs as well as up: the larder shelves were stored with seasonable fare, and every bit of copper and brass sparkled a welcome. Even the kitchen cat sported a ribbon, and had a specially energetic purr ready.

Into the midst of our happy preparations the bad news fell with bomb-like suddenness. The messenger who brought the telegram whistled shrilly and shuffled a breakdown on the doorstep while he waited to hear if there was an answer.

"He is ill. He can't come. Scarlet fever," one of us said in an odd, flat voice.

"Scarlet fever. At school. Oh! when can we go to him? When is there a boat?" cried the other.

There was no question of expediency. The Boy lay sick in a foreign land, so we went to him. It was full noon when the news came, and nightfall saw us dashing through the murk of a wild mid-December night towards Dover pier, feeling that only the express speed of the mail train was quick enough for us to breathe in.

But even the most apprehensive of journeys may hold its humours. Just at the moment of starting anxious friends assisted a young lady into our carriage. "She was going to Marseilles. Would we kindly see that she got on all right?" We were only going as far as Paris direct. "Well, then, as far as Paris. It would be a great favour." So from Charing Cross to the Gare du Nord, Placidia, as we christened her, became our care.

She was a large, handsome girl of about three-and-twenty. What was her reason for journeying unattended to Cairo we know not. Whether she ever reached her destination we are still in doubt, for a more complacently incapable damsel never went a-voyaging. The Saracen maiden who followed her English lover from the Holy Land by crying "London" and "À Becket" was scarce so impotent as Placidia; for any information the Saracen maiden had she retained, while Placidia naively admitted that she had already forgotten by which line of steamers her passage through the Mediterranean had been taken.

Placidia had an irrational way of losing her possessions. While yet on her way to the London railway station she had lost her tam-o'-shanter. So perforce, she travelled in a large picture-hat which, although pretty and becoming, was hardly suitable headgear for channel-crossing in mid-winter.

It was a wild night; wet, with a rising north-west gale. Tarpaulined porters swung themselves on to the carriage-steps as we drew up at Dover pier, and warned us not to leave the train, as, owing to the storm, the Calais boat would be an hour late in getting alongside.

The Ostend packet, lying beside the quay in full sight of the travellers, lurched giddily at her moorings. The fourth occupant of our compartment, a sallow man with yellow whiskers, turned green with apprehension. Not so Placidia. From amongst her chaotic hand-baggage she extracted walnuts and mandarin oranges, and began eating with an appetite that was a direct challenge to the Channel. Bravery or foolhardiness could go no farther.

Providence tempers the wind to the parents who are shorn of their lamb. The tumult of waters left us scatheless, but poor Placidia early paid the penalty of her rashness. She "thought" she was a good sailor—though she acknowledged that this was her first sea-trip—and elected to remain on deck. But before the harbour lights had faded behind us a sympathetic mariner supported her limp form—the feathers of her incongruous hat drooping in unison with their owner—down the swaying cabin staircase and deposited her on a couch.

"Oh! I do wish I hadn't eaten that fruit," she groaned when I offered her smelling-salts. "But then, you know, I was so hungry!"

In the train rapide a little later, Placidia, when arranging her wraps for the night journey, chanced, among the medley of her belongings, upon a missing boat-ticket whose absence at the proper time had threatened complications. She burst into good-humoured laughter at the discovery. "Why, here's the ticket that man made all the fuss about. I really thought he wasn't going to let me land till I found it. Now, I do wonder how it got among my rugs?"

We seemed to be awake all night, staring with wide, unseeing eyes out into the darkness. Yet the chill before dawn found us blinking sleepily at a blue-bloused porter who, throwing open the carriage door, curtly announced that we were in Paris.

Then followed a fruitless search for Placidia's luggage, a hunt which was closed by Placidia recovering her registration ticket (with a fragment of candy adhering to it) from one of the multifarious pockets of her ulster, and finding that the luggage had been registered on to Marseilles. "Will they charge duty on tobacco?" she inquired blandly, as she watched the Customs examination of our things. "I've such a lot of cigars in my boxes."

There was an Old-Man-of-the-Sea-like tenacity in Placidia's smiling impuissance. She did not know one syllable of French. A new-born babe could not have revealed itself more utterly incompetent. I verily believe that, despite our haste, we would have ended by escorting Placidia across Paris, and ensconcing her in the Marseilles train, had not Providence intervened in the person of a kindly disposed polyglot traveller. So, leaving Placidia standing the picture of complacent fatuosity in the midst of a group consisting of this new champion and three porters, we sneaked away.

Grey dawn was breaking as we drove towards St. Lazare Station, and the daily life of the city was well begun. Lights were twinkling in the dark interiors of the shops. Through the mysterious atmosphere figures loomed mistily, then vanished into the gloom. But we got no more than a vague impression of our surroundings. Throughout the interminable length of drive across the city, and the subsequent slow train journey, our thoughts were ever in advance.

The tardy winter daylight had scarcely come before we were jolting in a fiacre over the stony streets of Versailles. In the gutters, crones were eagerly rummaging among the dust heaps that awaited removal. In France no degradation attaches to open economies. Housewives on their way to fetch Gargantuan loaves or tiny bottles of milk for the matutinal café-au-lait cast searching glances as they passed, to see if among the rubbish something of use to them might not be lurking. And at one alluring mound an old gentleman of absurdly respectable exterior perfunctorily turned over the scraps with the point of his cane.

We had heard of a hotel, and the first thing we saw of it we liked. That was a pair of sabots on the mat at the foot of the staircase. Pausing only to remove the dust of travel, we set off to visit our son, walking with timorous haste along the grand old avenue where the school was situated. A little casement window to the left of the wide entrance-door showed a red cross. We looked at it silently, wondering.

In response to our ring the portal opened mysteriously at touch of the unseen concierge, and we entered. A conference with Monsieur le Directeur, kindly, voluble, tactfully complimentary regarding our halting French, followed. The interview over, we crossed the courtyard our hearts beating quickly. At the top of a little flight of worn stone steps was the door of the school hospital, and under the ivy-twined trellis stood a sweet-faced Franciscan Soeur, waiting to welcome us.

Passing through a tiny outer room—an odd combination of dispensary, kitchen, and drawing-room with a red-tiled floor—we reached the sick-chamber, and saw the Boy. A young compatriot, also a victim of the disease, occupied another bed, but for the first moments we were oblivious of his presence. Raising his fever-flushed face from the pillows, the Boy eagerly stretched out his burning hands.

"I heard your voices," his hoarse voice murmured contentedly, "and I knew you couldn't be ghosts." Poor child! in the semidarkness of the lonely night-hours phantom voices had haunted him. We of the morning were real.

The good Soeur buzzed a mild frenzy of "Il ne faut pas toucher" about our ears, but, all unheeding, we clasped the hot hands and crooned over him. After the dreary months of separation, love overruled wisdom. Mere prudence was not strong enough to keep us apart.

Chief amongst the chaos of thoughts that had assailed us on the reception of the bad news, was the necessity of engaging an English medical man. But at the first sight of the French doctor, as, clad in a long overall of white cotton, he entered the sick-room, our insular prejudice vanished, ousted by complete confidence; a confidence that our future experience of his professional skill and personal kindliness only strengthened.

It was with sore hearts that, the prescribed cinq minutes ended, we descended the little outside stair. Still, we had seen the Boy; and though we could not nurse him, we were not forbidden to visit him. So we were thankful too.

CHAPTER II
OGAMS

Our hotel was distinctively French, and immensely comfortable, in that it had gleaned, and still retained, the creature comforts of a century or two. Thus it combined the luxuries of hot-air radiators and electric light with the enchantment of open wood fires. Viewed externally, the building presented that airy aspect almost universal in Versailles architecture. It was white-tinted, with many windows shuttered without and heavily lace-draped within.

A wide entrance led to the inner courtyard, where orange trees in green tubs, and trelliswork with shrivelled stems and leaves still adhering, suggested that it would be a pleasant summer lounge. Our hotel boasted a grand salon, which opened from the courtyard. It was an elaborately ornate room; but on a chilly December day even a plethora of embellishment cannot be trusted to raise by a single degree the temperature of the apartment it adorns, and the soul turns from a cold hearth, however radiant its garnish of artificial blossoms. A private parlour was scarcely necessary, for, with most French bedrooms, ours shared the composite nature of the accommodation known in a certain class of advertisement as "bed-sitting-room." So it was that during these winter days we made ourselves at home in our chamber.

The shape of the room was a geometrical problem. The three windows each revealed different views, and the remainder of the walls curved amazingly. At first sight the furniture consisted mainly of draperies and looking-glass; for the room, though of ordinary dimensions, owned three large mirrors and nine pairs of curtains. A stately bed, endowed with a huge square down pillow, which served as quilt, stood in a corner. Two armchairs in brocaded velvet and a centre table were additions to the customary articles. A handsome timepiece and a quartette of begilt candelabra decked the white marble mantelpiece, and were duplicated in the large pier glass. The floor was of well-polished wood, a strip of bright-hued carpet before the bed, a second before the washstand, its only coverings. Need I say that the provision for ablutions was one basin and a liliputian ewer, and that there was not a fixed bath in the establishment?

It was a resting-place full of incongruities; but apart from, or perhaps because of, its oddities it had a cosy attractiveness. From the moment of our entrance we felt at home. I think the logs that purred and crackled on the hearth had much to do with its air of welcome. There is a sense of companionship about a wood fire that more enduring coal lacks. Like a delicate child, the very care it demands nurtures your affection. There was something delightfully foreign and picturesque to our town ideas in the heap of logs that Karl carried up in a great panier and piled at the side of the hearth. Even the little faggots of kindling wood, willow-knotted and with the dry copper-tinted leaves still clinging to the twigs, had a rustic charm.

These were pleasant moments when, ascending from the chill outer air, we found our chamber aglow with ruddy firelight that glinted in the mirrors and sparkled on the shining surface of the polished floor; when we drew our chairs up to the hearth, and, scorning the electric light, revelled in the beauty of the leaping and darting flames.

It was only in the salle-à-manger that we saw the other occupants of the hotel; and when we learned that several of them had lived en pension under the roof of the assiduous proprietor for periods varying from five to seven years, we felt ephemeral, mere creatures of a moment, and wholly unworthy of regard.

At eight o'clock Karl brought the petit déjeûner of coffee and rolls to our room. At eleven, our morning visit to the school hospital over, we breakfasted in the salle-à-manger, a large bright room, one or other of whose many south windows had almost daily, even in the depth of winter, to be shaded against the rays of the sun. Three chandeliers of glittering crystal starred with electric lights depended from the ceiling. Half a dozen small tables stood down each side; four larger ones occupied the centre of the floor, and were reserved for transient custom.

The first thing that struck us as peculiar was that every table save ours was laid for a single person, with a half bottle of wine, red or white, placed ready, in accordance with the known preference of the expected guest. We soon gathered that several of the regular customers lodged outside and, according to the French fashion, visited the hotel for meals only. After the early days of keen anxiety regarding our invalid had passed, we began to study our fellow guests individually and to note their idiosyncrasies. Sitting at our allotted table during the progress of the leisurely meals, we used to watch as one habitué after another entered, and, hanging coat and hat upon certain pegs, sat silently down in his accustomed place, with an unvarying air of calm deliberation.

Then Iorson, the swift-footed garçon, would skim over the polished boards to the newcomer, and, tendering the menu, would wait, pencil in hand, until the guest, after careful contemplation, selected his five plats from its comprehensive list.

The most picturesque man of the company had white moustaches of surprising length. On cold days he appeared enveloped in a fur coat, a garment of shaggy brown which, in conjunction with his hirsute countenance, made his aspect suggest the hero in pantomime renderings of "Beauty and the Beast." But in our hotel there was no Beauty, unless indeed it were Yvette, and Yvette could hardly be termed beautiful.

Yvette also lived outside. She did not come to déjeûner, but every night precisely at a quarter-past seven the farther door would open, and Yvette, her face expressing disgust with the world and all the things thereof, would enter.

Yvette was blonde, with neat little features, a pale complexion, and tiny hands that were always ringless. She rang the changes on half a dozen handsome cloaks of different degrees of warmth. To an intelligent observer their wear might have served as a thermometer. Yvette was blasée, and her millinery was in sympathy with her feelings. Her hats had all a fringe of disconsolate feathers, whose melancholy plumage emphasised the downward curve of her mouth. To see Yvette enter from the darkness and, seating herself at her solitary table, droop over her plate as though there were nothing in Versailles worth sitting upright for, was to view ennui personified.

Yvette invariably drank white wine, and the food rarely pleased her. She would cast a contemptuous look over the menu offered by the deferential Henri, then turn wearily away, esteeming that no item on its length merited even her most perfunctory consideration. But after one or two despondent glances, Yvette ever made the best of a bad bargain, and ordered quite a comprehensive little dinner, which she ate with the same air of utter disdain. She always concluded by eating an orange dipped in sugar. Even had a special table not been reserved for her, one could have told where Yvette had dined by the bowl of powdered sugar, just as one could have located the man with the fierce moustaches and the fur coat by the presence of his pepper-mill, or the place of "Madame" from her prodigal habit of rending a quarter-yard of the crusty French bread in twain and consuming only the soft inside.

From the ignorance of our cursory acquaintance we had judged the French a sociable nation. Our stay at Versailles speedily convinced us of the fallacy of that belief. Nothing could have impressed us so forcibly as did the frigid silence that characterised the company. Many of them had fed there daily for years, yet within the walls of the sunny dining-room none exchanged even a salutation. This unexpected taciturnity in a people whom we had been taught to regard as lively and voluble made us almost ashamed of our own garrulity, and when, in the presence of the silent company, we were tempted to exchange remarks, we found ourselves doing it in hushed voices as though we were in church.

A clearer knowledge, however, showed us that though some unspoken convention rendered the hotel guests oblivious of each other's presence while indoors, beyond the hotel walls they might hold communion. Two retired military men, both wearing the red ribbon of the Legion of Honour, as indeed did most of our habitués, sat at adjacent tables. One, tall and thin, was a Colonel; the other, little and neat, a Colonel also. To the casual gaze they appeared complete strangers, and we had consumed many meals in their society before observing that whenever the tall Colonel had sucked the last cerise from his glass of eau-de-vie, and begun to fold his napkin—a formidable task, for the serviettes fully deserved the designation later bestowed on them by the Boy, of "young table-cloths"—the little Colonel made haste to fold his also. Both rose from their chairs at the same instant, and the twain, having received their hats from the attentive Iorson, vanished, still mute, into the darkness together.

Once, to our consternation, the little Colonel replaced his napkin in its ring without waiting for the signal from the tall Colonel. But our apprehension that they, in their dealings in that mysterious outer world which twice daily they sought together, might have fallen into a difference of opinion was dispelled by the little Colonel, who had risen, stepping to his friend and holding out his hand. This the tall Colonel without withdrawing his eyes from Le Journal des Débats which he was reading, silently pressed. Then, still without a word spoken or a look exchanged, the little Colonel passed out alone.

The average age of the Ogams was seventy. True, there was Dunois the Young and Brave, who could not have been more than forty-five. What his name really was we knew not, but something in his comparatively juvenile appearance among the chevaliers suggested the appellation which for lack of a better we retained. Dunois' youth might only be comparative, but his bravery was indubitable; for who among the Ogams but he was daring enough to tackle the pâté-de-foie-gras, or the abattis, a stew composed of the gizzards and livers of fowls? And who but Dunois would have been so reckless as to follow baked mussels and crépinettes with rognons frits?

Dunois, too, revealed intrepid leanings toward strange liquors. Sometimes—it was usually at déjeûnerwhen he had dined out on the previous evening—he would demand the wine-list of Iorson, and rejecting the vin blanc or vin rouge which, being compris, contented the others, would order himself something of a choice brand. One of his favourite papers was Le Rire, and Henri, Iorson's youthful assistant, regarded him with admiration.

A less attractive presence in the dining-room was Madame. Madame, who was an elderly dame of elephantine girth, had resided in the hotel for half a dozen years, during which period her sole exercise had been taken in slowly descending from her chamber in the upper regions for her meals, and then, leisurely assimilation completed, in yet more slowly ascending. Madame's allotted seat was placed in close proximity to the hot-air register; and though Madame was usually one of the first to enter the dining-room, she was generally the last to leave. Madame's appetite was as animated as her body was lethargic. She always drank her half-bottle of red wine to the dregs, and she invariably concluded with a greengage in brandy. So it was small marvel that, when at last she left her chair to "tortoise" upstairs, her complexion should be two shades darker than when she descended.

Five dishes, irrespective of hors d'oeuvres at luncheon, and potage at dinner, were allowed each guest, and Madame's selection was an affair of time. Our hotel was justly noted for its cuisine, yet on infrequent occasions the food supplied to Madame was not to her mind. At these times the whole establishment suffered until the irascible old lady's taste was suited. One night at dinner Iorson had the misfortune to serve Madame with some turkey that failed to meet with her approval. With the air of an insulted empress, Madame ordered its removal. The conciliatory Iorson obediently carried off the dish and speedily returned, bearing what professed to be another portion. But from the glimpse we got as it passed our table we had a shrewd suspicion that Iorson the wily had merely turned over the piece of turkey and re-served it with a little more gravy and an additional dressing of cressons. Madame, it transpired, shared our suspicions, for this portion also she declined, with renewed indignation. Then followed a long period of waiting, wherein Madame, fidgeting restlessly on her seat, kept fierce eyes fixed on the door through which the viands entered.

Just as her impatience threatened to vent itself in action, Iorson appeared bearing a third helping of turkey. Placing it before the irate lady, he fled as though determined to debar a third repudiation. For a moment an air of triumph pervaded Madame's features. Then she began to gesticulate violently, with the evident intention of again attracting Iorson's notice. But the forbearance even of the diplomatic Iorson was at an end. Re-doubling his attentions to the diners at the farther side of the room, he remained resolutely unconscious of Madame's signals, which were rapidly becoming frantic.

The less sophisticated Henri, however, feeling a boyish interest in the little comedy, could not resist a curious glance in Madame's direction. That was sufficient. Waving imperiously, Madame compelled his approach, and, moving reluctantly, fearful of the issue, Henri advanced.

"Couteau!" hissed Madame. Henri flew to fetch the desired implement, and, realising that Madame had at last been satisfied, we again breathed freely.

A more attractive personage was a typical old aristocrat, officer of the Legion of Honour, who used to enter, walk with great dignity to his table, eat sparingly of one or two dishes, drink a glass of his vin ordinaire and retire. Sometimes he was accompanied by a tiny spaniel, which occupied a chair beside him; and frequently a middle-aged son, whose bourgeois appearance was in amazing contrast to that of his refined old father, attended him.

There were others, less interesting perhaps, but equally self-absorbed. One afternoon, entering the cable car that runs—for fun, apparently, as it rarely boasted a passenger—to and from the Trianon, we recognised in its sole occupant an Ogam who during the weeks of our stay had eaten, in evident oblivion of his human surroundings, at the table next to ours. Forgetting that we were without the walls of silence, we expected no greeting; but to our amazement he rose, and, placing himself opposite us, conversed affably and in most excellent English for the rest of the journey. To speak with him was to discover a courteous and travelled gentleman. Yet during our stay in Versailles we never knew him exchange even a bow with any of his fellow Ogams, who were men of like qualifications, though, as he told us, he had taken his meals in the hotel for over five years.

Early in the year our peace was rudely broken by the advent of a commercial man—a short, grey-haired being of an activity so foreign to our usage that a feeling of unrest was imparted to the salle-à-mangerthroughout his stay. His movements were distractingly erratic. In his opinion, meals were things to be treated casually, to be consumed haphazard at any hour that chanced to suit. He did not enter the dining-room at the exact moment each day as did the Ogams. He would rush in, throw his hat on a peg, devour some food with unseemly haste, and depart in less time than it took the others to reach the légumes.

He was hospitable too, and had a disconcerting way of inviting guests to luncheon or dinner, and then forgetting that he had done so. One morning a stranger entered, and after a brief conference with Iorson, was conducted to the commercial man's table to await his arrival. The regular customers took their wonted places, and began in their leisurely fashion to breakfast, and still the visitor sat alone, starting up expectantly every time a door opened, then despondently resuming his seat.

At last Iorson, taking compassion, urged the neglected guest to while away his period of waiting by trifling with the hors-d'oeuvres. He was proceeding to allay the pangs of hunger with selections from the tray of anchovies, sardines, pickled beet, and sliced sausage, when his host entered, voluble and irrepressible as ever. The dignified Ogams shuddered inwardly as his strident voice awoke the echoes of the room, and their already stiff limbs became rigid with disapproval.

In winter, transient visitors but rarely occupied one or other of the square centre tables, though not infrequently a proud father and mother who had come to visit a soldier son at the barracks, brought him to the hotel for a meal, and for a space the radiance of blue and scarlet and the glint of steel cast a military glamour over the staid company.

An amusing little circumstance to us onlookers was that although the supply of cooked food seemed equal to any demand, the arrival of even a trio of unexpected guests to dinner invariably caused a dearth of bread. For on their advent Iorson would dash out bareheaded into the night, to reappear in an incredibly short time carrying a loaf nearly as tall as himself.

One morning a stalwart young Briton brought to breakfast a pretty English cousin, on leave of absence from her boarding-school. His knowledge of French was limited. When anything was wanted he shouted "Garçon!" in a lordly voice, but it was the pretty cousin who gave the order. Déjeûner over, they departed in the direction of the Château. And at sunset as we chanced to stroll along the Boulevard de la Reine, we saw the pretty cousin, all the gaiety fled from her face, bidding her escort farewell at the gate of a Pension pour Demoiselles. The ball was over. Poor little Cinderella was perforce returning to the dust and ashes of learning.

CHAPTER III

THE TOWN

The English-speaking traveller finds Versailles vastly more foreign than the Antipodes. He may voyage for many weeks, and at each distant stopping-place find his own tongue spoken around him, and his conventions governing society. But let him leave London one night, cross the Channel at its narrowest—and most turbulent—and sunrise will find him an alien in a land whose denizens differ from him in language, temperament, dress, food, manners, and customs.

Of a former visit to Versailles we had retained little more than the usual tourist's recollection of a hurried run through a palace of fatiguing magnificence, a confusing peep at the Trianons, a glance around the gorgeous state equipages, an unsatisfactory meal at one of the open-aircafés, and a scamper back to Paris. But our winter residence in the quaint old town revealed to us the existence of a life that is all its own—a life widely variant, in its calm repose, from the bustle and gaiety of the capital, but one that is replete with charm, and abounding in picturesque-interest.

Versailles is not ancient; it is old, completely old. Since the fall of the Second Empire it has stood still. Most of the clocks have run down, as though they realised the futility of trying to keep pace with the rest of the world. The future merges into the present, the present fades into the past, and still the clocks of Versailles point to the same long eventide.

The proximity of Paris is evinced only by the vividly tinted automobiles that make Versailles their goal. Even they rarely tarry in the old town, but, turning at the Château gates, lose no time in retracing their impetuous flight towards a city whose usages accord better with their creed of feverish hurry-scurry than do the conventions of reposeful Versailles. And these fiery chariots of modernity, with their ghoulish, fur-garbed, and hideously spectacled occupants, once their raucous, cigale-like birr-r-r has died away in the distance, leave infinitely less impression on the placid life of Versailles than do their wheels on the roads they traverse. Under the grand trees of the wide avenues the townsfolk move quietly about, busying themselves with their own affairs and practising their little economies as they have been doing any time during the last century.

Perhaps it was the emphatic and demonstrative nature of the mourning worn that gave us the idea that the better-class female population of Versailles consisted chiefly of widows. When walking abroad we seemed incessantly to encounter widows: widows young and old, from the aged to the absurdly immature. It was only after a period of bewilderment that it dawned upon us that the sepulchral garb and heavy crape veils reaching from head to heel were not necessarily the emblems of widowhood, but might signify some state of minor bereavement. In Britain a display of black such as is an everyday sight at Versailles is undreamt of, and one saw more crape veils in a day in Versailles than in London in a week. Little girls, though their legs might be uncovered, had their chubby features shrouded in disfiguring gauze and to our unaccustomed foreign eyes a genuine widow represented nothing more shapely than a more or less stubby pillar festooned with crape.

But for an inborn conviction that a frugal race like the French would not invest in a plethora of mourning garb only to cast it aside after a few months' wear, and that therefore the period of wearing the willow must be greatly protracted, we would have been haunted by the idea that the adult male mortality of Versailles was enormous.

"Do they wear such deep mourning for all relatives?" I asked our hotel proprietor, who had just told us that during the first month of mourning the disguising veils were worn over the faces.

Monsieur shook his sleek head gravely, "But no, Madame, not for all. For a husband, yes; for a father or mother, yes; for a sister or brother, an uncle or aunt, yes; but for a cousin, no."

He pronounced the no so emphatically as almost to convince us of his belief that in refusing to mourn in the most lugubrious degree for cousins the Versaillese acted with praiseworthy self-denial.

There seemed to be no medium between sackcloth and gala-dress. We seldom noted the customary degrees of half-mourning. Plain colours were evidently unpopular and fancy tartans of the most flamboyant hues predominated amongst those who, during a spell of, say, three years had been fortunate enough not to lose a parent, sister, brother, uncle, or aunt. A perfectly natural reaction appeared to urge the ci-devantmourners to robe themselves in lively checks and tartans. It was as though they said—"Here at last is our opportunity for gratifying our natural taste in colours. It will probably be of but short duration. Therefore let us select a combination of all the most brilliant tints and wear them, for who knows how soon that gruesome pall of woe may again enshroud us."

Probably it was the vicinity of our hotel to the Church of Notre Dame that, until we discovered its brighter side, led us to esteem Versailles a veritable city of the dead, for on our bi-daily walks to visit the invalids we were almost certain to encounter a funeral procession either approaching or leaving Notre Dame. And on but rare occasions was the great central door undraped with the sepulchral insignia which proclaimed that a Mass for the dead was in prospect or in progress. Sometimes the sable valance and portières were heavily trimmed and fringed with silver; at others there was only the scantiest display of time-worn black cloth.

The humblest funeral was affecting and impressive. As the sad little procession moved along the streets—the wayfarers reverently uncovering and soldiers saluting as it passed—the dirge-like chant of the Miserere never failed to fill my eyes with unbidden tears of sympathy for the mourners, who, with bowed heads, walked behind the wreath-laden hearse.

Despite the abundant emblems of woe, Versailles can never appear other than bright and attractive. Even in mid-winter the skies were clear, and on the shortest days the sun seldom forgot to cast a warm glow over the gay, white-painted houses. And though the women's dress tends towards depression, the brilliant military uniforms make amends. There are 12,000 soldiers stationed in Versailles; and where a fifth of the population is gorgeous in scarlet and blue and gold, no town can be accused of lacking colour.

Next to the redundant manifestations of grief, the thing that most impressed us was the rigid economy practised in even the smallest details of expenditure. Among the lower classes there is none of that aping of fashion so prevalent in prodigal England; the different social grades have each a distinctive dress and are content to wear it. Among the men, blouses of stout blue cotton and sabots are common. Sometimes velveteen trousers, whose original tint years of wear have toned to some exquisite shade of heliotrope, and a russet coat worn with a fur cap and red neckerchief, compose an effect that for harmonious colouring would be hard to beat. The female of his species, as is the case in all natural animals, is content to be less adorned. Her skirt is black, her apron blue. While she is young, her neatly dressed hair, even in the coldest weather, is guiltless of covering. As her years increase she takes her choice of three head-dresses, and to shelter her grey locks selects either a black knitted hood, a checked cotton handkerchief, or a white cap of ridiculously unbecoming design.

No French workaday father need fear that his earnings will be squandered on such perishable adornments as feathers, artificial flowers, or ribbons. The purchases of his spouse are certain to be governed by extreme frugality. She selects the family raiment with a view to durability. Flimsy finery that the sun would fade, shoddy materials that a shower of rain would ruin, offer no temptations to her. When she expends a fewsous on the cutting of her boy's hair, she has it cropped until his cranium resembles the soft, furry skin of a mole, thus rendering further outlay in this respect unlikely for months. And when she buys a flannel shirt, a six-inch strip of the stuff, for future mending, is always included in the price.

But with all this economy there is an air of comfort, a complete absence of squalor. In cold weather the school-girls wear snug hoods, or little fur turbans; and boys have the picturesque and almost indestructible bérets of cloth or corduroy. Cloth boots that will conveniently slip inside sabots for outdoor use are greatly in vogue, and the comfortable Capuchin cloaks — whose peaked hood can be drawn over the head, thus obviating the use of umbrellas — are favoured by both sexes and all ages.

As may be imagined, little is spent on luxuries. Vendors of frivolities know better than to waste time tempting those provident people. On one occasion only did I see money parted with lightly, and in that case the bargain appeared astounding. One Sunday morning an enterprising huckster of gimcrack jewellery, venturing out from Paris, had set down his strong box on the verge of the market square, and, displaying to the admiring eyes of the country folks, ladies' and gentlemen's watches with chains complete, in the most dazzling of aureate metal, sold them at six sous apiece as quickly as he could hand them out.

Living is comparatively cheap in Versailles; though, as in all places where the cost of existence is low, it must be hard to earn a livelihood there. By far the larger proportion of the community reside in flats, which can be rented at sums that rise in accordance with the accommodation but are in all cases moderate. Housekeeping in a flat, should the owner so will it, is ever conducive to economy, and life in a French provincial town is simple and unconventional.

Bread, wine, and vegetables, the staple foods of the nation, are good and inexpensive. For 40 centimes one may purchase a bottle of vin de gard, a thin tipple, doubtless; but what kind of claret could one buy for fourpence a quart at home? Graves I have seen priced at 50 centimes, Barsac at 60, and eau de vie is plentiful at 1 franc 20!

Fish are scarce, and beef is supposed to be dear; but when butter, eggs, and cheese bulk so largely in the diet, the half chicken, the scrap of tripe, the slice of garlic sausage, the tiny cut of beef for the ragout, cannot be heavy items. Everything eatable is utilised, and many weird edibles are sold; for the French can contrive tasty dishes out of what in Britain would be thrown aside as offal.

On three mornings a week—Sunday, Tuesday, and Friday—the presence of the open-air market rouses Versailles from her dormouse-like slumber and galvanises her into a state of activity that lasts for several hours. Long before dawn, the roads leading townwards are busy with all manner of vehicles, from the great waggon drawn by four white horses driven tandem, and laden with a moving stack of hay, to the ramshackle donkey-cart conveying half a score of cabbages, a heap of dandelions grubbed from the meadows, and the owner.

By daybreak the market square under the leafless trees presents a lively scene. There are stalls sacred to poultry, to butter, eggs, and cheese; but the vegetable kingdom predominates. Flanked by bulwarks of greens and bundles of leeks of incredible whiteness and thickness of stem, sit the saleswomen, their heads swathed in gay cotton kerchiefs, and the ground before them temptingly spread with little heaps of corn salad, of chicory, and of yellow endive placed in adorable contrast to the scarlet carrots, blood-red beetroot, pinky-fawn onions, and glorious orange-hued pumpkins; while ready to hand are measures of white or mottled haricot beans, of miniature Brussels sprouts, and of pink or yellow potatoes, an esculent that in France occupies a very unimportant place compared with that it holds amongst the lower classes in Britain.

In Versailles Madame does her own marketing, her maid—in sabots and neat but usually hideous cap—accompanying her, basket laden. From stall to stall Madame passes, buying a roll of creamy butter wrapped in fresh leaves here, a fowl there, some eggs from the wrinkled old dame who looks so swart and witch-like in contrast to her stock of milk-white eggs.

Madame makes her purchases judiciously—time is not a valuable commodity in Versailles—and finishes, when the huge black basket is getting heavy even for the strong arms of the squat little maid, by buying a mess of cooked spinach from the pretty girl whose red hood makes a happy spot of colour among the surrounding greenery, and a measure of onions from the profound-looking sage who garners a winter livelihood from the summer produce of his fields.

Relations with uncooked food are, in Versailles, distinguished by an unwonted intimacy. No one, however dignified his station or appearance, is ashamed of purchasing the materials for his dinner in the open market, or of carrying them home exposed to the view of the world through the transpicuous meshes of a string bag. The portly gentleman with the fur coat and waxed moustaches, who looks a general at least, and is probably a tram-car conductor, bears his bunch of turnips with an air that dignifies the office, just as the young sub-lieutenant in the light blue cloak and red cap and trousers carries his mother's apples and lettuces without a thought of shame. And it is easy to guess the nature of the déjeûner of this simple soldat from the long loaf, the bottle of vin ordinaire, and the onions that form the contents of his net. In the street it was a common occurrence to encounter some non-commissioned officer who, entrusted with the catering for his mess, did his marketing accompanied by two underlings, who bore between them the great open basket destined to hold his purchases.

A picturesque appearance among the hucksters of the market square is the boîte de carton seller. Blue-bloused, with his stock of lavender or brown bandboxes strapped in a cardboard Tower of Pisa on his back, he parades along, his wares finding ready sale; for his visits are infrequent, and if one does not purchase at the moment, as does Madame, the opportunity is gone.

The spirit of camaraderie is strong amongst the good folks of the market. One morning the Artist had paused a moment to make a rough sketch of a plump, affable man who, shadowed by the green cotton awning of his stall, was selling segments of round flat cheeses of goat's milk; vile-smelling compounds that, judged from their outer coating of withered leaves, straw, and dirt, would appear to have been made in a stable and dried on a rubbish heap. The subject of the jotting, busy with his customers, was all unconscious; but an old crone who sat, her feet resting on a tiny charcoal stove, amidst a circle of decadent greens, detecting the Artist's action, became excited, and after eyeing him uneasily for a moment, confided her suspicions as to his ulterior motive to a round-faced young countryman who retailed flowers close by. He, recognising us as customers — even then we were laden with his violets and mimosa — merely smiled at her concern. But his apathy only served to heighten Madame's agitation. She was unwilling to leave her snug seat yet felt that her imperative duty lay in acquainting Monsieur du Fromage with the inexplicable behaviour of the inquisitive foreigner. But the nefarious deed was already accomplished, and as we moved away our last glimpse was of the little stove standing deserted, while Madame hastened across the street in her clattering sabots to warn her friend.

The bustle of the market is soon ended. By ten o'clock the piles of vegetables are sensibly diminished. By half-past ten the white-capped maid-servants have carried the heavy baskets home, and are busy preparing lunch. At eleven o'clock the sharp boy whose stock-in-trade consisted of three trays of snails stuffed à la Bourgogne has sold all the large ones at 45 centimes a dozen, all the small at 25, and quite two-thirds of the medium-sized at 35 centimes.

The clock points to eleven. The sun is high now. The vendors awaken to the consciousness of hunger, and Madame of the pommes fritesstall, whose assistant dexterously cuts the peeled tubers into strips, is fully occupied in draining the crisp golden shreds from the boiling fat and handing them over, well sprinkled with salt and pepper, to avid customers, who devour them smoking hot, direct from their paper cornucopias.

Long before the first gloom of the early mid-winter dusk, all has been cleared away. The rickety stalls have been demolished; the unsold remainder of the goods disposed of; the worthy country folks, their pockets heavy with sous, are well on their journey homewards, and only a litter of straw, of cabbage leaves and leek tops remains as evidence of the lively market of the morning.

CHAPTER IV

OUR ARBRE DE NOËL

We bought it on the Sunday morning from old Grand'mere Gomard in the Avenue de St. Cloud.

It was not a noble specimen of a Christmas-tree. Looked at with cold, unimaginative eyes, it might have been considered lopsided; undersized it undoubtedly was. Yet a pathetic familiarity in the desolate aspect of the little tree aroused our sympathy as no rare horticultural trophy ever could.

Some Christmas fairy must have whispered to Grand'mere to grub up the tiny tree and to include it in the stock she was taking into Versailles on the market morning. For there it was, its roots stuck securely into a big pot, looking like some forlorn forest bantling among the garden plants.

Grand'mere Gomard had established herself in a cosy nook at the foot of one of the great leafless trees of the Avenue. Straw hurdles were cunningly arranged to form three sides of a square, in whose midst she was seated on a rush-bottomed chair, like a queen on a humble throne. Her head was bound by a gaily striped kerchief, and her feet rested snugly on a charcoal stove. Her merchandise, which consisted of half a dozen pots of pink and white primulas, a few spotted or crimson cyclamen, sundry lettuce and cauliflower plants, and some roots of pansies and daisies, was grouped around her.

The primulas and cyclamen, though their pots were shrouded in pinafores of white paper skilfully calculated to conceal any undue lankiness of stem, left us unmoved. But the sight of the starveling little fir tree reminded us that in the school hospital lay two sick boys whose roseate dreams of London and holidays had suddenly changed to the knowledge that weeks of isolation and imprisonment behind the window-blind with the red cross lay before them. If we could not give them the longed-for home Christmas, we could at least give them a Christmas-tree.

The sight of foreign customers for Grand'mere Gomard speedily collected a small group of interested spectators. A knot of children relinquished their tantalising occupation of hanging round the pan of charcoal over whose glow chestnuts were cracking appetisingly, and the stall of the lady who with amazing celerity fried pancakes on a hot plate, and sold them dotted with butter and sprinkled with sugar to the lucky possessors of a sou. Even the sharp urchin who presided over the old red umbrella, which, reversed, with the ferule fixed in a cross-bar of wood, served as a receptacle for sheets of festive note-paper embellished with lace edges and further adorned with coloured scraps, temporarily entrusting a juvenile sister with his responsibilities, added his presence to our court.

Christmas-trees seemed not to be greatly in demand in Versailles, and many were the whispered communings as to what les Anglais proposed doing with the tree after they had bought it. When the transaction was completed and Grand'mere Gomard had exchanged the tree, with a sheet of La Patrie wrapped round its pot, for a franc and our thanks, the interest increased. We would require some one to carry our purchase, and each of the bright-eyed, short-cropped Jeans and Pierres was eager to offer himself. But our selection was already made. A slender boy in a béret and black pinafore, who had been our earliest spectator, was singled out and entrusted with the conveyance of the arbre de Noël to our hotel.

The fact that it had met with approbation appeared to encourage the little tree. The change may have been imaginary, but from the moment it passed into our possession the branches seemed less despondent, the needles more erect.

"Will you put toys on it?" the youthful porter asked suddenly.

"Yes; it is for a sick boy—a boy who has fever. Have you ever had an arbre de Noël?"

"Jamais," was his conclusive reply: the tone thereof suggesting that that was a felicity quite beyond the range of possibility.

The tree secured, there began the comparatively difficult work of finding the customary ornaments of glass and glitter to deck it. A fruitless search had left us almost in despair, when, late on Monday afternoon, we joyed to discover miniature candles of red, yellow, and blue on the open-air stall in front of a toy-store. A rummage in the interior of the shop procured candle clips, and a variety of glittering bagatelles. Laden with treasure, we hurried back to the hotel, and began the work of decoration in preparation for the morning.

During its short stay in our room at the hotel, the erstwhile despised little tree met with an adulation that must have warmed the heart within its rough stem. When nothing more than three coloured glass globes, a gilded walnut, and a gorgeous humming-bird with wings and tail of spun glass had been suspended by narrow ribbon from its branches, Rosine, the pretty Swiss chambermaid, chancing to enter the room with letters, was struck with admiration and pronounced it "très belle!"

And Karl bringing in a fresh panier of logs when the adorning was complete, and silly little delightful baubles sparkled and twinkled from every spray, putting down his burden, threw up his hands in amazement and declared the arbre de Noël "magnifique!"

This alien Christmas-tree had an element all its own. When we were searching for knick-knacks the shops were full of tiny Holy Babes lying cradled in waxen innocence in mangers of yellow corn. One of these little effigies we had bought because they pleased us. And when, the decoration of the tree being nearly finished, the tip of the centre stem standing scraggily naked called for covering, what more fitting than that the dear little Sacred Bébé in his nest of golden straw should have the place of honour?

It was late on Christmas Eve before our task was ended. But next morning when Karl, carrying in our petit déjeûner, turned on the electric light, and our anxious gaze sought our work, we found it good.

Then followed a hurried packing of the loose presents; and, a fiacre having been summoned, the tree which had entered the room in all humility passed out transmogrified beyond knowledge. Rosine, duster in hand, leant over the banisters of the upper landing to watch its descent. Karl saw it coming and flew to open the outer door for its better egress. Even the stout old driver of the red-wheeled cab creaked cumbrously round on his box to look upon its beauties.

The Market was busy in the square as we rattled through. From behind their battlemented wares the country mice waged wordy war with the town mice over the price of merchandise. But on this occasion we were too engrossed to notice a scene whose picturesque humour usually fascinated us, for as the carriage jogged over the rough roads the poor little arbre de Noël palpitated convulsively. The gewgaws clattered like castanets, as though in frantic expostulation, and the radiant spun-glass humming-birds quivered until we expected them to break from their elastic fetters and fly away. The green and scarlet one with the gold-flecked wings fell on the floor and rolled under the seat just as the cab drew up at the great door of the school.

The two Red-Cross prisoners who, now that the dominating heat of fever had faded, were thinking wistfully of the forbidden joys of home, had no suspicion of our intention, and we wished to surprise them. So, burdened with our treasure, we slipped in quietly.

From her lodge window the concierge nodded approval. And at the door of the hospital the good Soeur received us, a flush of pleasure glorifying her tranquil face.

Then followed a moment wherein the patients were ordered to shut their eyes, to reopen them upon the vision splendid of the arbre de Noël. Perhaps it was the contrast to the meagre background of the tiny school-hospital room, with its two white beds and bare walls, but, placed in full view on the centre table, the tree was almost imposing. Standing apart from Grand'mere's primulas and cyclamen as though, conscious of its own inferiority, it did not wish to obtrude, it had looked dejected, miserable. During its sojourn at the hotel the appreciation of its meanness had troubled us. But now, in the shabby little chamber, where there were no rival attractions to detract from its glory, we felt proud of it. It was just the right size for the surroundings. A two-franc tree, had Grand'mere possessed one, would have been Brobdignagian and pretentious.

A donor who is handicapped by the knowledge that the gifts he selects must within a few weeks be destroyed by fire, is rarely lavish in his outlay. Yet our presents, wrapped in white paper and tied with blue ribbons, when arranged round the flower-pot made a wonderful show, There were mounted Boers who, when you pressed the ball at the end of the air-tube, galloped in a wobbly, uncertain fashion. The invalids had good fun later trying races with them, and the Boy professed to find that his Boer gained an accelerated speed when he whispered "Bobs" to him. There were tales of adventure and flasks of eau-de-Cologne and smart virile pocket-books, one red morocco, the other blue. We regretted the pocket-books; but their possession made the recipients who, boylike, took no heed for the cleansing fires of the morrow, feel grown-up at once. And they yearned for the advent of the first day of the year, that they might begin writing in their new diaries. For the Sister there was a miniature gold consecrated medal. It was a small tribute of our esteem, but one that pleased the devout recipient.

Suspended among the purely ornamental trinkets of the tree hung tiny net bags of crystallised violets and many large chocolates rolled up in silver paper. The boys, who had subsisted for several days on nothing more exciting than boiled milk, openly rejoiced when they caught sight of the sweets. But to her patients' disgust, the Soeur, who had a pretty wit of her own, promptly frustrated their intentions by counting the dainties.

"I count the chocolates. They are good boys, wise boys, honest boys, and I have every confidence in them, but—I count the chocolates!" said the Soeur.

As we passed back along the Rue de la Paroisse, worshippers were flocking in and out of Notre Dame, running the gauntlet of the unsavoury beggars who, loudly importunate, thronged the portals. Before the quiet nook wherein, under a gold-bestarred canopy, was the tableau of the Infant Jesus in the stable, little children stood in wide-eyed adoration, and older people gazed with mute devotion.

Some might deem the little spectacle theatrical, and there was a slight irrelevance in the pot-plants that were grouped along the foreground, but none could fail to be impressed by the silent reverence of the congregation. No service was in process, yet many believers knelt at prayer. Here a pretty girl returned thanks for evident blessings received; there an old spinster, the narrowness of whose means forbade her expending a couple of sous on the hire of a chair, knelt on the chilly flags and murmured words of gratitude for benefits whereof her appearance bore no outward indication.

We had left the prisoners to the enjoyment of their newly acquired property in the morning. At gloaming we again mounted the time-worn outside stair leading to the chamber whose casement bore the ominous red cross. The warm glow of firelight filled the room, scintillating in the glittering facets of the baubles on the tree; and from their pillows two pale-faced boys—boys who, despite their lengthening limbs were yet happily children at heart—watched eager-eyed while the sweet-faced Soeur, with reverential care, lit the candles that surrounded the HolyBébé.

CHAPTER V

LE JOUR DE L'ANNÉE

The closing days of 1900 had been unusually mild. Versailles townsfolk, watching the clear skies for sign of change, declared that it would be outside all precedent if Christmas week passed without snow. But, defiant of rule, sunshine continued, and the new century opened cloudless and bright.

Karl, entering with hot water, gave us seasonable greeting, and as we descended the stair, pretty Rosine, brushing boots at the open window of the landing, also wished us a smiling bonne nouvelle année. But within or without there was little token of gaiety. Sundry booths for the sale of gingerbread and cheapjouets, which had been erected in the Avenue de St. Cloud, found business languishing, though a stalwart countryman in blouse and sabots, whose stock-in-trade consisted of whirligigs fashioned in the semblance of moulins rouges and grotesque blue Chinamen which he carried stuck into a straw wreath fixed on a tall pole, had no lack of custom.

The great food question never bulks so largely in the public interest as at the close of a year, so perhaps it was but natural that the greatest appreciation of the festive traditions of the season should be evinced by the shops devoted to the sale of provender. Turkeys sported scarlet bows on their toes as though anticipating a dance rather than the oven; and by their sides sausages, their somewhat plethoric waists girdled by pink ribbon sashes, seemed ready to join them in the frolic. In one cookshop window a trio of plaster nymphs who stood ankle-deep in a pool of crimped green paper, upheld a huge garland of cunningly moulded wax roses, dahlias, and lilac, above which perched a pheasant regnant. This trophy met with vast approbation until a rival establishment across the way, not to be outdone, exhibited a centrepiece of unparalleled originality, consisting as it did of a war scene modelled entirely in lard. Entrenched behind the battlements of the fort crowning an eminence, Boers busied themselves with cannon whose aim was carefully directed towards the admiring spectators outside the window, not at the British troops who were essaying to scale the greasy slopes. Half way up the hill, a miniature train appeared from time to time issuing from an absolutely irrelevant tunnel, and, progressing at the rate of quite a mile an hour, crawled into the corresponding tunnel on the other side. At the base of the hill British soldiers, who seemed quite cognisant of the utter futility of the Boer gunnery, were complacently driving off cattle. Captious critics might have taken exception to the fact that the waxen camellias adorning the hill were nearly as big as the battlements, and considerably larger than the engine of the train. But fortunately detractors were absent, and such trifling discrepancies did not lessen the genuine delight afforded the spectators by this unique design which, as a card proudly informed the world, was entirely the work of the employés of the firm.

It was in a pâtisserie in the Rue de la Paroisse that we noticed an uninviting compound labelled "Pudding Anglais, 2 fr. 1/2 kilo." A little thought led us to recognise in this amalgamation a travesty of our old friend plum-pudding; but so revolting was its dark, bilious-looking exterior that we felt its claim to be accounted a compatriot almost insulting. And it was with secret gratification that towards the close of January we saw the same stolid, unhappy blocks awaiting purchasers.

The presence of the customary Tuesday market kept the streets busy till noon. But when the square was again empty of sellers and buyers Versailles relapsed into quietude. I wonder if any other town of its size is as silent as Versailles. There is little horse-traffic. Save for the weird, dirge-like drone of the electric cars, which seems in perfect consonance with the tone of sadness pervading the old town whose glory has departed, the clang of the wooden shoes on the rough pavement, and the infrequent beat of hoofs as a detachment of cavalry moves by, unnatural stillness seems to prevail.

Of street music there was none, though once an old couple wailing a plaintive duet passed under our windows. Britain is not esteemed a melodious nation, yet the unclassical piano is ever with us, and even in the smallest provincial towns one is rarely out of hearing of the insistent note of some itinerant musician. And no matter how far one penetrates into the recesses of the country, he is always within reach of some bucolic rendering of the popular music-hall ditty of the year before last. But never during our stay in Versailles, a stay that included what is supposedly the gay time of the year, did we hear the sound of an instrument, or — with the one exception of the old couple, whom it would be rank flattery to term vocalists — the note of a voice raised in song.

With us, New Year's Day was a quiet one. A dozen miles distant, Paris was welcoming the advent of the new century in a burst of feverish excitement. But despite temptations, we remained in drowsy Versailles, and spent several of the hours in the little room where two pallid Red-Cross knights, who were celebrating the occasion by sitting up for the first time, waited expectant of our coming as their one link with the outside world.

It was with a sincere thrill of pity that at déjeûner we glanced round the salle-à-manger and found all the Ogams filling their accustomed solitary places. Only Dunois the comparatively young, and presumably brave, was absent. The others occupied their usual seats, eating with their unfailing air of introspective absorption. Nobody had cared enough for these lonely old men to ask them to fill a corner at their tables, even on New Year's Day. To judge by their regular attendance at the hotel meals, these men — all of whom, as shown by their wearing the red ribbon of the Legion of Honour, had merited distinction — had little hospitality offered them. Most probably they offered as little, for, throughout our stay, none ever had a friend to share his breakfast or dinner.

The bearing of the hotel guests suggested absolute ignorance of one another's existence. The Colonels, as I have said in a previous chapter, were exceptions, but even they held intercourse only without the hotel walls. Day after day, month after month, year after year as we were told, these men had fed together, yet we never saw them betray even the most cursory interest in one another. They entered and departed without revealing, by word or look, cognisance of another human being's presence. Could one imagine a dozen men of any other nationality thus maintaining the same indifference over even a short period? I hope future experience will prove me wrong, but in the meantime my former conception of the French as a nation overflowing with bonhomie and camaraderie is rudely shaken.

The day of the year would have passed without anything to distinguish it from its fellows had not the proprietor, who, by the way, was a Swiss, endeavoured by sundry little attentions to reveal his goodwill. Oysters usurped the place of the customary hors d'oeuvres at breakfast, and the meal ended with café noir and cognac handed round by the deferential Iorson as being "offered by the proprietor," who, entering during the progress of the déjeûner, paid his personal respects to his clientèle.

The afternoon brought us a charming discovery. We had a boy guest with us at luncheon, a lonely boy left at school when his few compatriots—save only the two Red-Cross prisoners—had gone home on holiday. The day was bright and balmy; and while strolling in the park beyond the Petit Trianon, we stumbled by accident upon the hameau, the little village of counterfeit rusticity wherein Marie Antoinette loved to play at country life.

Following a squirrel that sported among the trees, we had strayed from the beaten track, when, through the leafless branches, we caught sight of roofs and houses and, wandering towards them, found ourselves by the side of a miniature lake, round whose margin were grouped the daintiest rural cottages that monarch could desire or Court architect design.

History had told us of the creation of this unique plaything of the capricious Queen, but we had thought of it as a thing of the past, a toy whose fragile beauty had been wrecked by the rude blows of the Revolution. The matter-of-fact and unromantic Baedeker, it is true, gives it half a line. After devoting pages to the Château, its grounds, pictures, and statues, and detailing exhaustively the riches of the Trianons, he blandly mentions the gardens of the Petit Trianon as containing "some fine exotic trees, an artificial lake, a Temple of Love, and a hamlet where the Court ladies played at peasant life."

It is doubtful whether ten out of every hundred tourists who, Baedeker in hand, wander conscientiously over the grand Château—Palace, alas! no longer—ever notice the concluding words, or, reading its lukewarm recommendation, deem the hamlet worthy of a visit. The Château is an immense building crammed with artistic achievements, and by the time the sightseer of ordinary capacity has seen a tenth of the pictures, a third of the sculpture, and a half of the fountains, his endurance, if not all his patience, is exhausted.

I must acknowledge that we, too, had visited Versailles without discovering that the hameau still existed; so to chance upon it in the sunset glow of that winter evening seemed to carry us back to the time when the storm-cloud of the Revolution was yet no larger than a man's hand; to the day when Louis XVI., making for once a graceful speech, presented the site to his wife, saying: "You love flowers. Ah! well, I have a bouquet for you—the Petit Trianon." And his Queen, weary of the restrictions of Court ceremony—though it must be admitted that the willful Marie Antoinette ever declined to be hampered by convention—experiencing in her residence in the little house freedom from etiquette, pursued the novel pleasure to its furthest by commanding the erection in its grounds of a village wherein she might the better indulge her newly fledged fancy for make-believe rusticity.

About the pillars supporting the verandah-roof of the chief cottage and that of the wide balcony above, roses and vines twined lovingly. And though it was the first day of January, the rose foliage was yet green and bunches of shrivelled grapes clung to the vines. It was lovely then; yet a day or two later, when a heavy snowfall had cast a white mantle over the village, and the little lake was frozen hard, the scene seemed still more beautiful in its ghostly purity.

At first sight there was no sign of decay about the long-deserted hamlet. The windows were closed, but had it been early morning, one could easily have imagined that the pseudo villagers were asleep behind the shuttered casements, and that soon the Queen, in some charming déshabillé, would come out to breathe the sweet morning air and to inhale the perfume of the climbing roses on the balcony overlooking the lake, wherein gold-fish darted to and fro among the water-lilies; or expect to see the King, from the steps of the little mill where he lodged, exchange blithe greetings with the maids of honour as they tripped gaily to the laiterie to play at butter-making, or sauntered across the rustic bridge on their way to gather new-laid eggs at the farm.

The sunset glamour had faded and the premature dusk of mid-winter was falling as, approaching nearer, we saw where the roof-thatch had decayed, where the insidious finger of Time had crumbled the stone walls. A chilly wind arising, moaned through the naked trees. The shadow of the guillotine seemed to brood oppressively over the scene, and, shuddering, we hastened away.

CHAPTER VI
ICE-BOUND

Even in the last days of December rosebuds had been trying to open on the standard bushes in the sheltered rose-garden of the Palace. But with the early nights of January a sudden frost seized the town in its icy grip, and, almost before we had time to realise the change of weather, pipes were frozen and hot-water bottles of strange design made their appearance in the upper corridors of the hotel. The naked cherubs in the park basins stood knee-deep in ice, skaters skimmed the smooth surface of the canal beyond the tapis vert, and in a twinkling Versailles became a town peopled by gnomes and brownies whose faces peeped quaintly from within conical hoods.

Soldiers drew their cloak-hoods over their uniform caps. Postmen went their rounds thus snugly protected from the weather. The doddering old scavengers, plying their brooms among the great trees of the avenues, bore so strong a resemblance to the pixies who lurk in caves and woods, that we almost expected to see them vanish into some crevice in the gnarled roots of the trunks. Even the tiny acolytes trotting gravely in the funeral processions had their heads and shoulders shrouded in the prevailing hooded capes.

To us, accustomed though we were to an inclement winter climate, the chill seemed intense. So frigid was the atmosphere that the first step taken from the heated hotel hall into the outer air felt like putting one's face against an iceberg. All wraps of ordinary thickness appeared incapable of excluding the cold, and I sincerely envied the countless wearers of the dominant Capuchin cloaks.

Our room was many-windowed, and no matter how high Karl piled the logs, nor how close we sat to the flames, our backs never felt really warm. It was only when night had fallen and the outside shutters were firmly closed that the thermometer suspended near the chimney-piece grudgingly consented to record temperate heat.

But there was at least one snug chamber in Versailles, and that was the room of the Red-Cross prisoners. However extravagant the degrees of frost registered without, the boys' sick-room was always pleasantly warm. How the good Soeur, who was on duty all day, managed to regulate the heat throughout the night-watches was her secret. A half-waking boy might catch a glimpse of her, apparently robed as by day, stealing out of the room; but so noiseless were her movements, that neither of the invalids ever saw her stealing in. They had a secret theory that in her own little apartment, which was just beyond theirs, the Soeur, garbed, hooded, and wearing rosary and the knotted rope of her Order, passed her nights in devotion. Certain it was that even the most glacial of weathers did not once avail to prevent her attending the Mass that was held at Notre Dame each morning before daybreak.

Frost-flowers dulled the inner glories of the shop windows with their unwelcome decoration. Even in the square on market mornings business flagged. The country folks, chilled by their cold drive to town, cowered, muffled in thick wraps, over their little charcoal stoves, lacking energy to call attention to their wares. The sage with the onions was absent, but the pretty girl in the red hood held her accustomed place, warming mittened fingers at a chaufferette which she held on her lap. The only person who gave no outward sign of misery was the boulangère who, harnessed to her heavy hand-cart, toiled unflinchingly on her rounds.

In the streets the comely little bourgeoises hid their plump shoulders under ugly black knitted capes, and concealed their neat hands in clumsy worsted gloves. But despite the rigour of the atmosphere their heads, with the hair neatly dressed à la Chinoise, remained uncovered. It struck our unaccustomed eyes oddly to see these girls thus exposed, standing on the pavement in the teeth of some icy blast, talking to stalwart soldier friends, whose noses were their only visible feature.

The ladies of Versailles give a thought to their waists, but they leave their ankles to Providence, and any one having experience of Versailles winter streets can fully sympathise with their trust; for even in dry sunny weather mud seems a spontaneous production that renders goloshes a necessity.

And when frost holds the high-standing city in its frigid grasp the extreme cold forbids any idea of coquetry, and thickly lined boots with cloth uppers—a species of foot-gear that in grace of outline is decidedly suggestive of "arctics"—become the only comfortable wear.

After a few days of thought-congealing cold—a cold so intense that sundry country people who had left their homes before dawn to drive into Paris with farm produce were taken dead from their market-carts at the end of the journey—the weather mercifully changed. A heavy snowfall now tempered the inclement air, and turned the leafless park into a fairy vision.

The nights were still cold, but during the day the sun glinted warmly on the frozen waters of the gilded fountains and sparkled on the facets of the crisp snow. The marble benches in the sheltered nooks of the snug Château gardens were occupied by little groups, which usually consisted of a bonne and a baby, or of a chevalier and a hopelessly unclassable dog; for the dogs of Versailles belong to breeds that no man living could classify, the most prevalent type in clumsiness of contour and astonishing shagginess of coat resembling nothing more natural than those human travesties of the canine race familiar to us in pantomime.

Along the snow-covered paths under the leafless trees, on whose branches close-wreathed mistletoe hangs like rooks' nests, the statues stood like guardian angels of the scene. They had lost their air of aloofness and were at one with the white earth, just as the forest trees in their autumn dress of brown and russet appear more in unison with their parent soil than when decked in their bravery of summer greenery.

CHAPTER VII
THE HAUNTED CHATEAU

The Château of Versailles, like the town, dozes through the winter, only half awakening on Sunday afternoons when the townsfolk make it their meeting-place. Then conscripts, in clumsy, ill-fitting uniforms, tread noisily over the shining parqueterie floors, and burgesses gossip amicably in the dazzling Galerie des Glaces, where each morning courtiers were wont to await the uprising of their king. But on the weekdays visitors are of the rarest. Sometimes a few half-frozen people who have rashly automobiled thither from Paris alight at the Château gates, and take a hurried walk through the empty galleries to restore the circulation to their stiffened limbs before venturing to set forth on the return journey.

Every weekday in the Place d'Armes, squads of conscripts are busily drilling, running hither and thither with unflagging energy, and the air resounds with the hoarse staccato cries of "Un! Deux! Trois!" wherewith they accompany their movements, cries that, heard from a short distance, exactly resemble the harsh barking of a legion of dogs.

Within the gates there is a sense of leisure: even the officials have ceased to anticipate visitors. In the Cour Royale two little girls have cajoled an old guide into playing a game of ball. A custodian dozes by the great log fire in the bedroom of Louis XIV., where the warm firelight playing on the rich trappings lends such an air of occupation to the chamber, that—forgetting how time has turned to grey the once white ostrich plumes adorning the canopy of the bed, and that the priceless lace coverlet would probably fall to pieces at a touch—one almost expects the door to open for the entrance of Louis le Grand himself.

To this room he came when he built the Palace wherein to hide from that grim summons with which the tower of the Royal sepulture of St. Denis, visible from his former residence, seemed to threaten him. And here it was that Death, after long seeking, found him. We can see the little great-grandson who was to succeed, lifted on to the bed of the dying monarch.

"What is your name, my child?" asks the King.

"Louis XV;" replies the infant, taking brevet-rank. And nearly sixty years later we see the child, his wasted life at an end, dying of virulent smallpox under the same roof, deserted by all save his devoted daughters.

To me the Palace of Versailles is peopled by the ghosts of many women. A few of them are dowdy and good, but by far the greater number are graceful and wicked. How infinitely easier it is to make a good bad reputation than to achieve even a bad good one! "Tell us stories about naughty children," we used to beseech our nurses. And as our years increase we still yawn over the doings of the righteous, while our interest in the ways of transgressors only strengthens.

We all know by heart the romantic lives of the shrinking La Vallière, of Madame de Montespan the impassioned, of sleek Madame de Maintenon—the trio of beauties honoured by the admiration of Louis le Grand; and of the bevy of favourites of Louis XV, the three fair and short-lived sisters de Mailly-Nesle, the frail Pompadour who mingled scheming with debauchery, and the fascinating but irresponsible Du Barry. Even the most minute details of Marie Antoinette's tragic career are fresh in our memories, but which of us can remember the part in the history of France played by Marie Leczinska? Yet, apart from her claim to notability as having been the last queen who ended her days on the French throne, her story is full of romantic interest.

Thrusting aside the flimsy veil of Time, we find Marie Leczinska the penniless daughter of an exiled Polish king who is living in retirement in a dilapidated commandatory at a little town in Alsace. It is easy to picture the shabby room wherein the unforeseeing Marie sits content between her mother and grandmother, all three diligently broidering altar cloths. Upon the peaceful scene the father enters, overcome by emotion, trembling. His face announces great news, before he can school his voice to speak.

"Why, father! Have you been recalled to the throne of Poland?" asks Marie, and the naïve question reveals that many years of banishment have not quenched in the hearts of the exiles the hope of a return to their beloved Poland.

"No, my daughter, but you are to be Queen of France," replies the father. "Let us thank God."

Knowing the sequel, one wonders if it was for a blessing or a curse that the refugees, kneeling in that meagre room in the old house at Wissenberg, returned thanks.

Certain it is that the ministers of the boy-monarch were actuated more by a craving to further their own ends than either by the desire to please God or to honour their King, in selecting this obscure maiden from the list of ninety-nine marriageable princesses that had been drawn up at Versailles. A dowerless damsel possessed of no influential relatives is not in a position to be exacting, and, whate'er befell, poor outlawed Stanislas Poniatowski could not have taken up arms in defence of his daughter.

Having a sincere regard for unaffected Marie Leczinska, I regret being obliged to admit that, even in youth, "comely" was the most effusive adjective that could veraciously be awarded her. And it is only in the lowest of whispers that I will admit that she was seven years older than her handsome husband, whose years did not then number seventeen. Yet is there indubitable charm in the simple grace wherewith Marie accepted her marvellous transformation from pauper to queen. She disarmed criticism by refusing to conceal her former poverty. "This is the first time in my life I have been able to make presents," she frankly told the ladies of the Court, as she distributed among them her newly got trinkets.

It is pleasant to remember that the early years of her wedded life passed harmoniously. Louis, though never passionately enamoured of his wife, yet loved her with the warm affection a young man bestows on the first woman he has possessed. And that Marie was wholly content there is little doubt. She was no gadabout. Versailles satisfied her. Three years passed before she visited Paris, and then the visit was more of the nature of a pilgrimage than of a State progress. Twin daughters had blessed the union, and the Queen journeyed to the churches of Notre Dame and Saint Geneviève to crave from Heaven the boon of a Dauphin: a prayer which a year later was answered.

But clouds were gathering apace. As he grew into manhood the domestic virtues palled upon Louis. He tired of the needlework which, doubtless, Marie's skilled hands had taught him. We recall how, sitting between her mother and grandmother, the future Queen had broidered altar cloths. Marie Leczinska was an adoring mother; possibly her devotion to their rapidly increasing family wearied him. Being little more than a child himself, the King is scarcely likely to have found the infantile society so engaging as did the mother. Thus began that series of foolish infidelities that, characterised by extreme timidity and secrecy at first, was latterly flaunted in the face of the world.

Marie's life was not a smooth one, but it was happier than that of her Royal spouse. To me there is nothing sadder, nothing more sordid in history, than the feeble, useless existence of Louis XV., whose early years promised so well. It is pitiful to look at the magnificent portrait, still hanging in the palace where he reigned, of the child-king seated in his robes of State, the sceptre in his hand, looking with eyes of innocent wonder into the future, then to think upon the depth of degradation reached by the once revered Monarch before his body was dragged in dishonour and darkness to its last resting-place.

Pleasanter figures that haunt the Château are those of the six pretty daughters of Louis and Marie Leczinska. There are the ill-starred twins, Elizabeth and Henrietta: Madame Elizabeth, who never lost the love of her old home, and, though married, before entering her teens, to the Infanta of Spain, retired, after a life of disappointment, to her beloved Versailles to die; and the gentle Henrietta who, cherishing an unlucky passion for the young Duc de Chartres, pined quietly away after witnessing her lover wed to another.

Then there is Adelaide, whom Nattier loved to paint, portraying her sometimes as a lightly clad goddess, sometimes sitting demurely in a pretty frock. Good Nattier! there is a later portrait of himself in complacent middle age surrounded by his wife and children; but I like to think that, when he spent so many days at the Palace painting the young Princess, some tenderer influence than mere artistic skill lent cunning to his brush.

When the daughters of Louis XV. were sent to be educated at a convent, Adelaide it was who, by tearful protest to her royal father, gained permission to remain at the Palace while her sisters meekly endured their banishment. From this instance of childish character one would have anticipated a career for Madame Adelaide, and I hate being obliged to think of her merely developing into one of the three spinster aunts of Louis XVI. who, residing under the same roof, turned coldly disapproving eyes upon the manifold frailties of their niece, Marie Antoinette.

The sisters Victoire and Sophie are faint shades leaving no impression on the memory; but there is another spirit, clad in the sombre garb of a Carmelite nun, who, standing aloof, looks with the calm eyes of peace on the motley throng. It is Louise, the youngest sister of all, who, deeply grieved by her father's infatuation for the Du Barry—an infatuation which, beginning within a month of Marie Leczinska's decease, ended only when on his deathbed the dying Monarch prepared to receive absolution by bidding his inamorata farewell—resolved to flee her profligate surroundings and devote her life to holiness.

It is affecting to think of the gentle Louise, secretly anticipating the rigours of convent life, torturing her delicate skin by wearing coarse serge, and burning tallow candles in her chamber to accustom herself to their detestable odour.

Her father's consent gained, Louise still tarried at Versailles. Perhaps the King's daughter shrank from voluntarily beginning a life of imprisoned drudgery. We know that at this period she passed many hours reading contemporary history, knowing that, once within the convent walls, the study of none but sacred literature would be permitted.

Then came an April morning when Louise, who had kept her intention secret from all save her father, left the Palace never to return. France, in a state of joyous excitement, was eagerly anticipating the arrival of Marie Antoinette, who was setting forth on the first stage of that triumphal journey which had so tragic an ending. Already the gay clamour of wedding-bells filled the air; and Louise may have feared that, did she linger at Versailles, the enticing vanities of the world might change the current of her thoughts.

Chief among the impalpable throng that people the state galleries is Marie Antoinette, and her spirit shows us many faces. It is charming, haughty, considerate, headstrong, frivolous, thoughtful, degraded, dignified, in quick succession. We see her arrive at the Palace amid the tumultuous adoration of the crowd, and leave amidst its execrations. Sometimes she is richly apparelled, as befits a queen; anon she sports the motley trappings of a mountebank. The courtyard that saw the departure of Madame Louise witnesses Marie Antoinette, returning at daybreak in company with her brother-in-law from some festivity unbecoming a queen, refused admittance by the King's express command.

Many of the attendant spirits who haunt Marie Antoinette's ghostly footsteps as they haunted her earthly ones are malefic. Most are women, and all are young and fair. There is Madame Roland, who, taken as a young girl to the Palace to peep at the Royalties, became imbued by that jealous hatred which only the Queen's death could appease.

"If I stay here much longer," she told that kindly mother who sought to give her a treat by showing her Court life, "I shall detest these people so much that I shall be unable to hide my hatred."

It is easy to fancy the girl's evil face scowling at the unconscious Queen, before she leaves to pen those inflammatory pamphlets which are to prove the Sovereign's undoing and her own. For by some whim of fate Madame Roland was executed on the very scaffold to which her envenomed writings had driven Marie Antoinette.

A spectre that impresses as wearing rags under a gorgeous robe, lurks among the foliage of the quietbosquet beyond the orangerie. It is the infamous Madame de la Motte, chief of adventuresses, and it was in that secluded grove that her tool, Cardinal de Rohan, had his pretended interview with the Queen. Poor, perfidious Contesse! what an existence of alternate beggarly poverty and beggarly riches was hers before that last scene of all when she lay broken and bruised almost beyond human semblance in that dingy London courtyard beneath the window from which, in a mad attempt to escape arrest, she had thrown herself.

Through the Royal salons flits a presence whereat the shades of the Royal Princesses look askance: that of the frolicsome, good-natured, irresponsible Du Barry. A soulless ephemera she, with no ambitions or aspirations, save that, having quitted the grub stage, she desires to be as brilliant a butterfly as possible. Close in attendance on her moves an ebon shadow — Zamora, the ingrate foundling who, reared by the Duchesse, swore that he would make his benefactress ascend the scaffold, and kept his oath. For our last sight of the prodigal, warm-hearted Du Barry, plaything of the aged King, is on the guillotine, where in agonies of terror she fruitlessly appeals to her executioner's clemency.

But of all the bygone dames who haunt the grand Château, the only one I detest is probably the most irreproachable of all — Madame de Maintenon. There is something so repulsively sanctimonious in her aspect, something so crafty in the method wherewith, under the cloak of religion, she wormed her way into high places, ousting — always in the name of propriety — those who had helped her. Her stepping-stone to Royal favour was handsome, impetuous Madame de Montespan, who, taking compassion on her widowed poverty, appointed Madame Scarron, as she then was, governess of her children, only to find her protégée usurp her place both in the honours of the King and in the affections of their children.

The natural heart rebels against the "unco guid," and Madame de Maintenon, with her smooth expression, double chin, sober garments and ever-present symbols of piety, revolts me. I know it is wrong. I know that historians laud her for the wholesome influence she exercised upon the mind of a king who had grown timorous with years; that the dying Queen declared that she owed the King's kindness to her during the last twenty years of her life entirely to Madame de Maintenon. But we know also that six months after the Queen's death an unwonted light showed at midnight in the Chapel Royal, where Madame de Maintenon — the child of a prison cell — was becoming the legal though unacknowledged wife of Louis XIV. The impassioned, uncalculating de Montespan had given the handsome

Monarch her all without stipulation. Truly the career of Madame de Maintenon was a triumph of virtue over vice; and yet of all that heedless, wanton throng, my soul detests only her.

CHAPTER VIII

MARIE ANTOINETTE

Stereotyped sights are rarely the most engrossing. At the Palace of Versailles the petits appartements de la Reine, those tiny rooms whose grey old-world furniture might have been in use yesterday, to me hold more actuality than all the regal salons in whose vast emptiness footsteps reverberate like echoes from the past.

In the pretty sitting-room the coverings to-day are a reproduction of the same pale blue satin that draped the furniture in the days when queens preferred the snug seclusion of those dainty rooms overlooking the dank inner courtyard to the frigid grandeur of their State chambers. Therein it was that Marie Leczinska was wont to instruct her young daughters in the virtues as she had known them in her girlhood's thread-bare home, not as her residence at the profligate French Court had taught her to understand them.

The heavy gilt bolts bearing the interlaced initials M.A. remind us that these, too, were the favourite rooms of Marie Antoinette, and that in all probability the cunningly entwined bolts were the handiwork of her honest spouse, who wrought at his blacksmith forge below while his wife flirted above. But in truth the petits appartements are instinct with memories of Marie Antoinette, and it is difficult to think of any save only her occupying them. The beautiful coffre presented to her with the layette of the Dauphin still stands on a table in an adjoining chamber, and the paintings on its white silk casing are scarcely faded yet, though the decorative ruching of green silk leaves has long ago fallen into decay.

A step farther is the little white and gold boudoir which still holds the mirror that gave the haughty Queen her first premonition of the catastrophe that awaited her. Viewed casually the triple mirror, lining an alcove wherein stands a couch garlanded with flowers, betrays no sinister qualities. But any visitor who approaches looking at his reflection where at the left the side panels meet the angle of the wall, will be greeted by a sight similar to that whose tragic suggestion made even the haughty Queen pause a moment in her reckless career. For in the innocent appearing mirrors the gazer is reflected without a head.

It was through this liliputian suite, this strip of homeliness so artfully introduced into a palace, that Marie Antoinette fled on that fateful August morning when the mob of infuriated women invaded the Château.

Knowing this, I was puzzling over the transparent fact that either of the apparent exits would have led her directly into the hands of the enemy, when the idea of a secret staircase suggested itself. A little judicious inquiry elicited the information that one did exist. "But it is not seen. It is locked. To view it, an order from the Commissary—that is necessary," explained the old guide.

To know that a secret staircase, and one of such vivid historical importance, was at hand, and not to have seen it would have been too tantalising. The "Commissary" was an unknown quantity, and for a space it seemed as though our desire would be ungratified. Happily the knowledge of our interest awoke a kindly reciprocity in our guide, who, hurrying off, quickly returned with the venerable custodian of the key. A moment later, the unobtrusive panel that concealed the exit flew open at its touch, and the secret staircase, dark, narrow, and hoary with the dust of years, lay before us.

Many must have been the romantic meetings aided by those diminutive steps, but, peering into their shadows, we saw nothing but a vision of Marie Antoinette, half clad in dishevelled wrappings of petticoat and shawl, flying distracted from the vengeance of the furies through the refuge of the low-roofed stairway.

In my ingenuous youth, when studying French history, I evolved a theory which seemed, to myself at least, to account satisfactorily for the radical differences distinguishing Louis XVI. from his brothers and antecedents. Finding that, when a delicate infant, he had been sent to the country to nurse, I rushed to the conclusion that the royal infant had died, and that his foster-mother, fearful of the consequences, had substituted a child of her own in his place. The literature of the nursery is full of instances that seemed to suggest the probability of my conjecture being correct.

As a youth, Louis had proved himself both awkward and clumsy. He was loutish, silent in company, ill at ease in his princely surroundings, and in all respects unlike his younger brothers. He was honest, sincere, pious, a faithful husband, a devoted father; amply endowed, indeed, with the middle-class virtues which at that period were but rarely found in palaces. To my childish reasoning the most convincing proof lay in his innate craving for physical labour; a craving that no ridicule could dispel.

With the romantic enthusiasm of youth, I used to fancy the peasant mother stealing into the Palace among the spectators who daily were permitted to view the royal couple at dinner, and imagine her, having seen the King, depart glorying secretly in the strategy that had raised her son to so high an estate. There was another picture, in whose dramatic misery I used to revel. It showed the unknown mother, who had discovered that by her own act she had condemned her innocent son to suffer for the sins of past generations of royal profligates, journeying to Paris (in my dreams she always wore sabots and walked the entire distance in a state of extreme physical exhaustion) with the intention of preventing his execution by declaring his lowly parentage to the mob. The final tableau revealed her, footsore and weary, reaching within sight of the guillotine just in time to see the executioner holding up her son's severed head. I think my imaginary heroine died of a broken heart at this juncture, a catastrophe that would naturally account for her secret dying with her.

During our winter stay at Versailles, my childish phantasies recurred to me, and I almost found them feasible. What an amazing irony of fate it would have shown had a son of the soil expired to expiate the crimes of sovereigns!

But more pitiful by far than the saddest of illusions is the sordid reality of a scene indelibly imprinted on my mental vision. Memory takes me back to the twilight of a spring Sunday several years ago, when in the wake of a cluster of market folks we wandered into the old Cathedral of St. Denis. Deep in the sombre shadows of the crypt a light gleamed faintly through a narrow slit in the stone wall. Approaching, we looked into a gloomy vault wherein, just visible by the ray of a solitary candle, lay two zinc coffins.

Earth holds no more dismal sepulchre than that dark vault, through the crevice in whose wall the blue-bloused marketers cast curious glances. Yet within these grim coffins lie two bodies with their severed heads, all that remains mortal of the haughty Marie Antoinette and other humble spouse.

CHAPTER IX
THE PRISONERS RELEASED

The first dread days, when the Boy, heavy with fever, seemed scarcely to realise our presence, were swiftly followed by placid hours when he lay and smiled in blissful content, craving nothing, now that we were all together again. But this state of beatitude was quickly ousted by a period of discontent, when the hunger fiend reigned supreme in the little room.

"Manger, manger, manger, tout le temps!" Thus the nurse epitomised the converse of her charges. And indeed she was right, for, from morning till night, the prisoners' solitary topic of conversation was food. During the first ten days their diet consisted solely of boiled milk, and as that time wore to a close the number of quarts consumed increased daily, until Paul, the chief porter, seemed ever ascending the little outside stair carrying full bottles of milk, or descending laden with empty ones.

"Milk doesn't count. When shall we be allowed food, real food?" was the constant cry, and their relief was abounding when, on Christmas Day, the doctor withdrew his prohibition, and permitted an approach to the desired solids. But even then the prisoners, to their loudly voiced disappointment, discovered that their only choice lay between vermicelli and tapioca, nursery dishes which at home they would have despised.

"Tapioca! Imagine tapioca for a Christmas dinner!" the invalids exclaimed with disgust. But that scorn did not prevent them devouring the mess and eagerly demanding more. And thereafter the saucepan simmering over the gas-jet in the outer room seemed ever full of savoury spoon-meat.

I doubt if any zealous mother-bird ever had a busier time feeding her fledglings than had the good Sister in satisfying the appetites of these callow cormorants. To witness the French nun seeking to allay the hunger of these voracious schoolboy aliens was to picture a wren trying to fill the ever-gaping beaks of two young cuckoos whom an adverse fate had dropped into her nest.

As the days wore by, the embargo placed upon our desire to cater for the invalids was gradually lifted, and little things such as sponge biscuits and pears crept in to vary the monotony of the milk diet.

New Year's Day held a tangible excitement, for that morning saw a modified return to ordinary food, and, in place of bottles of milk, Paul's load consisted of such tempting selections from the school meals as were deemed desirable for the invalids. Poultry not being included in the school menus, we raided a cooked-provision shop and carried off a plump, well-browned chicken. The approbation which met this venture resulted in our supplying a succession of poulettes, which, at the invalids' express desire, were smuggled into their room under my cloak. Not that there was the most remote necessity for concealment, but the invalids, whose sole interest centred in food, laboured under the absurd idea that, did the authorities know they were being supplied from without, their regular meals would be curtailed to prevent them over-eating.

The point of interest, for the Red-Cross prisoners at least, in our morning visits lay in the unveiling of the eatables we had brought. School food, however well arranged, is necessarily stereotyped, and the element of the unknown ever lurked in our packages. The sugar-sticks, chocolates, fruit, little cakes, or what we had chanced to bring, were carefully examined, criticised, and promptly devoured.

A slight refreshment was served them during our short stay, and when we departed we left them eagerly anticipating luncheon. At gloaming, when we returned, it was to find them busy with half-yards of the long crusty loaves, plates of jelly, and tumblers, filled with milk on our Boy's part, and with well diluted wine on that of his fellow sufferer.

Fear of starvation being momentarily averted, the Soeur used to light fresh candles around the tiny Holy Bébé on the still green Christmas-tree, and for a space we sat quietly enjoying the radiance. But by the time the last candle had flickered out, and the glow of a commonplace paraffin lamp lighted the gloom, nature again demanded nourishment; and we bade the prisoners farewell for the night, happy in the knowledge that supper, sleep, and breakfast would pleasantly while away the hours till our return.

The elder Red-Cross knight was a tall, good-looking lad of sixteen, the age when a boy wears painfully high collars, shaves surreptitiously—and unnecessarily—with his pen-knife, talks to his juniors about the tobacco he smokes in a week, and cherishes an undying passion for a maiden older than himself. He was ever an interesting study, though I do not think I really loved him until he confided his affairs of the heart, and entrusted me with the writing of his love-letters. I know that behind my back he invariably referred to me as "Ma"; but as he openly addressed the unconscious nun as "you giddy old girl," "Ma" might almost be termed respectful, and I think our regard was mutual.

All things come to him who waits. There came a night when for the last time we sat together around the little tree, watching the Soeur light the candles that illuminated the Holy Bébé. On the morrow the prisoners, carefully disinfected, and bearing the order of their release in the form of a medical certificate, would be set free.

It clouded our gladness to know that before the patient Sister stretched another period of isolation. Just that day another pupil had developed scarlet fever, and only awaited our boys' departure to occupy the little room. Hearing that this fresh prisoner lay under sentence of durance vile, we suggested that all the toys—chiefly remnants of shattered armies that, on hearing of the Boy's illness, we had brought from the home playroom he had outgrown—might be left for him instead of being sent away to be burnt.

The Boy's bright face dulled. "If it had been anybody else! But, mother, I don't think you know that he is the one French boy we disliked. It was he who always shouted 'à bas les Anglais!' in the playground."

The reflection that for weary weeks this obnoxious boy would be the only inmate of the boîte, as the invalids delighted to call their sick-room, overcame his antipathetic feeling, and he softened so far as to indite a polite little French note offering his late enemy his sympathy, and formally bequeathing to him the reversion of his toys, including the arbre de Noël with all its decorations, except the little waxen Jesus nestling in the manger of yellow corn; the Soeur had already declared her intention of preserving that among her treasures.

The time that had opened so gloomily had passed, and now that it was over we could look back upon many happy hours spent within the dingy prison walls. And our thoughts were in unison, for the Boy, abruptly breaking the silence, said: "And after all, it hasn't been such a bad time. Do you know, I really think I've rather enjoyed it!"

L'ENVOI

Heavy skies lowered above us, the landscape seen through the driving mist-wreaths showed a depressing repetition of drabs and greys as we journeyed towards Calais. But, snugly ensconced in the train rapide, our hearts beat high with joy, for at last were we homeward bound. The weeks of exile in the stately old town had ended. For the last time the good Sister had lit us down the worn stone steps. As we sped seawards across the bleak country, our thoughts flew back to her, and to the little room with the red cross on its casement, wherein, although our prisoners were released, another term of nursing had already begun for her. In contrast with her life of cheerful self-abnegation, ours seemed selfish, meaningless, and empty.

Dear nameless Sister! She had been an angel of mercy to us in a troublous time, and though our earthly paths may never again cross, our hearts will ever hold her memory sacred.

www.ingramcontent.com/pod-product-compliance
Lightning Source LLC
Chambersburg PA
CBHW081628100526
44590CB00021B/3648